Theosophy and the Conscious Mind

Theosophy and the Conscious Mind

Texts by
Pablo Sender &
H. P. Blavatsky

martin firrell company
MODERN THEOSOPHY

First published in 2020 by Martin Firrell Company Ltd
10 Queen Street Place, London EC4R 1AG, United Kingdom.

ISBN 978-1-912622-24-5

Text is set in Baskerville, 12pt on 18pt.

Baskerville is a serif typeface designed in 1754 by John Baskerville
(1706–1775) in Birmingham, England. Compared to earlier typeface
designs, Baskerville increased the contrast between thick and thin
strokes. Serifs were made sharper and more tapered, and the axis of
rounded letters was placed in a more vertical position. The curved
strokes were made more circular in shape, and the characters became
more regular.

Baskerville is categorised as a transitional typeface between classical
typefaces and high contrast modern faces. Of his own typeface, John
Baskerville wrote, 'Having been an early admirer of the beauty of
letters, I became insensibly desirous of contributing to the perfection
of them. I formed to myself ideas of greater accuracy than had yet
appeared, and had endeavoured to produce a set of types according to
what I conceived to be their true proportion.'

Introduction
by Moon Laramie

In this edition of the Modern Theosophy series, Pablo Sender and H.P. Blavatsky examine the nature of consciousness. In Pablo Sender's view, 'Perhaps the fundamental problem for humanity, the root of all our woes, is that we don't know who we really are. Theosophical teachings shed light on this fundamental issue...' According to H.P. Blavatsky, Theosophy is 'the philosophy of a reasoned and scientific mysticism'.

Gottfried de Purucker's *Occult Glossary* states that 'consciousness is the finest and loftiest form of energy, is the root of all things, and is coextensive with kosmic space... the universe therefore is imbodied consciousness'.[1]

In Theosophy, the concept of Atman is pivotal to an understanding of consciousness. Both Sender and Blavatsky describe Atman as an all-pervading 'conscious non-consciousness'. Blavatsky maintains that Atman 'contains everything, the potentiality of all; therefore, it is nothing and all.' Sender defines Atman as 'the spiritual, psychological and physical space in which everything (including us) takes place and has its being'.

The next principle of consciousness after

Atman is Buddhi. Pablo Sender observes that, for Theosophists, 'We can think of it as the way in which the absolute Atman first appears in the world of differentiation... Buddhi should be regarded as the first principle of sentiency in the cosmos. The possibility of sentient beings exists because of Buddhi.' But there is no sense of individuality. Consciousness without individuality exists in the animal, vegetable and mineral kingdoms. All three embody varying degrees of conscious life energy, but none are self-conscious.

Only human beings are consciously self-aware. This self-awareness can be seen in humanity's search for answers to fundamental existential questions. As Sender explains, 'A special feature of human beings is the presence of an individuality or Ego... This conscious sense of being does not come from Atman or Buddhi but from Manas....'

Human beings often consider themselves as separate from the rest of the universe. According to the Theosophical author E.L. Gardner, 'Compared with the freedom of the Archetypal Consciousness in which life has its rise, the limitations imposed by the normal physical body make it a veritable prison-house.'[2] This physicality is an illusion. Pablo Sender argues, 'At the level of our highest nature we are the whole, not a fragment of reality... the Manasic self-awareness (or self-consciousness) has a higher expression in the *impersonal sense of being*, and a lower one in the *personal sense of identity*.'

Ultimately, individual human consciousness remains part of the one universal consciousness. As Annie Besant puts it, 'Consciousness is a unit, and the divisions we make in it are either made for purposes of study, or are illusions, due to the limitation of our perceptive power by the organs through which it works in the lower worlds... It is, of course, true that there is but One Self in the fullest sense of the words; that as rays flame forth from the sun, the Selves that are the true Men are but rays of the Supreme Self, and that each Self may whisper; *I am He*.'[3]

Both H.P. Blavatsky and Pablo Sender identify a path of spiritual as well as physical evolution that humanity must tread. E.L. Gardner notes that, 'For many the first step on the upward evolutionary path is the clear knowledge of a higher and a lower, an inner and an outer self, that is to say, a distinction between the divine spark and its abode, and an understanding of their relationship.'[4] This presents a challenge for a human race so caught up in the physical world. As the occultist and Theosophist C. Jinarajadasa remarks, 'The first great marvel about consciousness is that the whole is in the part, the total is in the unit.'[5]

1. G. de Purucker, *Occult Glossary*, Rider and Co. London, 1933. Note: 'Imbody' is an archaic form of 'embody'.

2. E.L. Gardner, *The Play of Consciousness Within The Web*, Theosophical Publishing House, 1939.

3. Annie Besant, *Thought Power*, Theosophical Publishing Society, 1901.

4. E.L. Gardner, *The Play of Consciousness Within The Web*, Theosophical Publishing House, 1939.

5. C. Jinarajadasa, *First Principles of Theosophy*, Theosophical Publishing House, 1922.

Pablo Sender

Pablo Sender was born in Argentina in 1975. He was raised a Catholic and from a young age he was interested in spirituality. Exploring a range of New Age philosophies, he developed a strong belief in reincarnation.

He trained originally as a molecular biologist and holds a doctorate in Biological Sciences. This field appealed to him because he 'wanted to know how life works'. He was particularly interested in molecular biology and the structure and mechanics of DNA. While studying for his degree, he became increasingly interested in philosophy and began to explore the work of different philosophers in his spare time.

Pablo joined the Theosophical Society in Argentina in 1996 when he was 21 years old. He was drawn to Theosophy because 'it presented a far wider scope of knowledge' than studying science alone.

In 2005, he travelled to Southern India and stayed for two years at the International Headquarters of the Theosophical Society in Adyar, Chennai. He worked at the society's archives during Radha Burnier's presidency.

He later moved to the United States to live and work at the National Center of the Theosophical Society in America (TSA), in Wheaton, Illinois. He contributed to the development of the Theosophical Society's wiki and supported the society's education and outreach programmes for nine years.

Pablo is a prolific lecturer and leads classes, seminars, and retreats around the world, both in Spanish and English. He has taught courses on H.P. Blavatsky and her seminal work, *The Secret Doctrine*. He describes *The Secret Doctrine* as 'a book that is not so much descriptive but that gives you hints of a reality that is beyond words.' He sees Theosophy as 'a way of challenging my views and trying to reach a truer view than the one I had. There is a deeper view that allows you to relate to the world and to yourself in a better way. Theosophy is about constantly questioning your current view and trying to discover a higher view.'

He believes Theosophy frees the individual from the limitations of spiritual dogma. 'You can explore different spiritual approaches that are meaningful to you, personally, without being limited by rigid outside influences.'

He is the author of *Evolution of the Higher Consciousness. An In-depth Study of H.P. Blavatsky's Teachings* (www.fohatproductions.com, 2018).

Pablo Sender lives in Ojai, California with his wife, Michele. He continues to work for the TSA, as well as the Krotona Institute of Theosophy.

The Nature of the Monad
by Pablo Sender (2020)

When we look at the deeper aspects of Theosophy, we can appreciate the unique ability it has to open new vistas on the nature of life and human beings. Perhaps the fundamental problem for humanity, the root of all our woes, is that we don't know who we really are. Theosophical teachings shed light on this fundamental issue and, if we strive to assimilate their meaning, they can lend invaluable support in facing the challenges that life brings.

The limitations of words

Before we explore the teachings about our true nature it is important to understand the limitations of words. Metaphysical truths cannot really be conveyed by oral or written means. Words are an intellectual device created to describe a particular perception of the world - that of the physical reality, but when we try to move beyond that realm, they fail to bring to mind the true meaning of what we are trying to communicate. For this reason, Blavatsky said that words and symbols, though necessary for gaining a preliminary understanding, must ultimately be transcended:

'Once define an idea in words, and it loses its reality; once figure a metaphysical idea, and you materialize its spirit. Figures must be used only as ladders to scale the battlements, ladders to be disregarded once the foot is set upon the rampart.'[1]

Since written or spoken statements about the higher worlds are subject to this limitation, various philosophies arrive at different views on the nature of Truth. In Buddhism, for example, the ultimate reality is described as non-self - 'Anatman' in Sanskrit. Hinduism, on the other hand, states that the ultimate reality is pure self, Atman. According to Blavatsky, both assertions are true and not true at the same time, because the ultimate reality is neither 'self' nor 'non-self' as we understand them. Indeed, the various terms we might use to state a metaphysical truth may be more or less appropriate to express some aspects of it, but will fail to express others. Therefore, when examining fundamental questions, we need to do it from multiple perspectives, otherwise our understanding will be lopsided.

According to Blavatsky, the esoteric philosophy she learned from her Masters has its own terminology, but these terms are not available to the public at large. This left her with two alternatives when trying to convey her knowledge - either she needed to devise new terms, or to use existing ones, applying them in specific ways to suit her teachings. She chose the latter approach, which is what most philosophers and spiritual teachers do. For example, in Western philosophy, Kant[2] used the term 'intuition' in a way that suited his own particular philosophical concept, but other philosophers have used the same word to indicate different concepts entirely. Blavatsky leaned towards the use of ancient languages (Sanskrit primarily) to translate her technical terms because they are better suited than modern languages to transmit the metaphysical ideas she wanted to share.

Atman - the Higher Self

Blavatsky frequently described human beings as consisting of seven principles or aspects. The seventh or highest principle is Atman, which she described as being a ray of the Absolute. Atman is in fact the presence of the ultimate reality in human beings.

It is impossible to describe the Absolute in relative terms. In religion, deities tend to be endowed with the good qualities people are expected to develop, while the bad qualities are often embodied in a separate entity, such as the Devil. But this division can only take place in the world of duality. The ultimate reality must encompass everything; there can be nothing outside of the Absolute. If, for example, one were to say that the Absolute is blue, it would mean that it is not red, or yellow; but this would imply that red and yellow are outside the absolute reality, which is not possible. Similarly, stating that the Absolute is eternal love would imply the impossible notion that hate lies outside the Absolute. Can we then say that the ultimate reality is both love and hate? Can we say that it is both blue, red, and yellow? Obviously not. Since everything that exists is an expression of the Absolute, the latter must contain the *potentiality* of everything - in an *undifferentiated state*. Using the analogy of light and colours, we could say that the Absolute is like the white light, which contains the potentiality of all the colours without being any of them in particular. The first point to keep in mind, then, is that Atman - being a ray of the Absolute - cannot be defined by any finite quality.

According to Blavatsky, her teachers belonged to the Buddhist tradition, or rather, to an esoteric aspect of it, not to the popular religion known to the masses. Yet, when referring to the ultimate reality in us, Blavatsky uses the word 'Atman', which seems to be more consistent with Hindu teachings. When we examine the way Blavatsky defined Atman, however, we see that it is actually quite in accord with the Buddhist concept of 'Anatman' or 'non-self'. In fact, the use of the word 'Atman' in Theosophy can lead to a misunderstanding. It may steer people to regard their atmic nature from a Hindu perspective, i.e., '*My* Atman is *my* Higher Self, and everybody else has their own Atman.' But this is not the true teaching and it is important to understand why.

In *The Secret Doctrine Commentaries*, Blavatsky states, 'Atman is nothing. It is all absolute and it cannot be said that it is this, that or the other. It is simply that in which we are, we live and breathe and have our being.' The idea here is that Atman is an omnipresent principle, not a particular subject or object that you can point to. In fact, Blavatsky relates Atman to *space* - the spiritual, psychological and physical space in which everything (including us) takes place and has its being. Now, we must keep in mind that, from an esoteric perspective, space is not a void. Space is the potentiality of everything - the ground from which emerge consciousness, matter, and energy.

From the previous quote it should be clear that Atman is not really a human principle. As Blavatsky explains, it is 'a universal principle in which Man[3] participates, but so does equally every physical and subjective atom, and also every blade of grass and everything that lives or is in Space whether it is sensible of it or not.'[4] One can therefore say that a stone, an ant, or an angel, are all rooted in Atman just as much as we are.

It should also be obvious that Atman is not an *individual* principle. This is why in *The Secret Doctrine Commentaries* Blavatsky says, 'You must never say my Atman. You have no Atman. This idea is the curse of the world.' This statement resembles what the Buddha taught; he said that there is no permanent Atman (self) in a human being. This is usually taken to mean that there is no Atman at all, but according to Blavatsky this interpretation is wrong. She maintains that the Buddha's teaching was that there is no permanent Atman as an *individual* principle, which is not to say that there is no Self as a common universal principle.

Blavatsky maintained that the idea of having our own Atman is a curse. 'It has produced this tremendous selfishness. This egotism. We say we are my Atman, my Buddhi. Who are you? You are nobody, you are something today and tomorrow you are not.' Thinking that there is in me a permanent distinct self means that, ultimately speaking, 'I' am different and separate from 'you'. Theosophical teachings state the opposite. At the level of our highest nature we are the whole, not a fragment of reality. Clinging to the idea of being a separate fragment of reality is the cause of all the strife we see in the world, including ambition, aggression and conflict.

A way to visualize our individuality in the context of unity would be to think of our bodies as particular centres through which the *universal* Atman is expressing itself. As Blavatsky said, Atman 'is in

Metaphysics, that point in space which the human Monad and its vehicle, man, occupy for the period of every life'.[5] The Vedanta school of Hinduism uses the following image to describe this idea: we talk about the space inside a jar and the space outside of it, but in truth there aren't two separate spaces - this is an illusion created by the walls of the jar. Break the jar and you find that there is only one space. Similarly, when the universal Atman is experienced through a particular centre of consciousness, we have an 'individual experience' of Atman although there is not really an 'individual Atman'.

Let us now examine Atman in terms of consciousness. Being a ray of the Absolute, the seventh principle could be defined as 'absolute consciousness.' It is important to note, however, that even though we may use this phrase as a description, we don't really know what it means. We may think that the absolute consciousness is similar to ours - only larger, but this would be a mistake. In *The Secret Doctrine*, Blavatsky says that consciousness as we know it 'implies limitations and qualifications'. You always need an *object* separate from the *subject*, who is conscious of that object. Thus, when describing consciousness, there is always the duality between the subject and the object, plus the *perception* that brings them in touch. 'But Absolute Consciousness,' she explains, 'contains the cognizer, the thing cognized and the cognition, all three in itself and all three one.' This is evidently not the kind of consciousness we normally experience.

Blavatsky elaborates further, 'Understand me, Atman cannot [even] be called infinite consciousness. It is the one Absolute, which is *conscious non-consciousness*. It contains everything, the potentiality of all; therefore, it is nothing and all.' The term 'conscious non-consciousness' is an appropriate description of Atman because it sits between the two extremes. At one end, we may regard Atman as unconsciousness, in much the same way many Buddhists regard Nirvana as an annihilation - but Blavatsky says Atman is conscious. At the other end, we may imagine Atman as a blissful extension of our dualistic consciousness, just as those Christians who imagine heaven as a glorified extension of physical reality - but Blavatsky says that Atman is non-consciousness. The term 'conscious non-consciousness', then, points to the truth that Atman is not consciousness as we know it, but it is not merely unconsciousness. By contemplating and approaching this intuitively we can grasp a sense of what this might mean, while avoiding the common misapprehensions that religions have fallen into when trying to describe the higher realities with objective terms.

Buddhi - the Spiritual Soul

The second higher principle in human beings is called 'Buddhi'. We can think of it as the way in which the absolute Atman first appears in the world of differentiation. In Blavatsky's words, 'Atman is said to have Buddhi for a vehicle, because Buddhi is already the first differentiation after the evolution of the universe.'[6] Let us use an analogy to understand the relationship between these two principles. Picture a sheet of paper. If you take the sheet to represent the universe, Atman would be the space in which the paper exists, while Buddhi could be viewed as the paper itself. This paper is the 'original substance' on which all kinds of things can be drawn; it is the substratum existing in space.

Anything drawn or written on the sheet has space and paper as its basis. To make this analogy more accurate, we should think of the paper as a temporary condensation of space - a visible manifestation of the invisible and boundless space.

Buddhi *Atman*

Buddhi is still on a plane of unity and can have no qualities like the ones we know in the world of duality. As Blavatsky says, 'It is simply the vehicle of Atman, of spirit, and spirit is nothing.'[7] Here, by 'nothing' she means 'no thing'; 'nothing in particular' that our lower mind can perceive. She adds, 'It cannot be said it is something. It is that which has neither beginning nor end. It is the one thing.' Buddhi is the one homogeneous source of everything that exists at the manifested level. Returning to the example of light and colour, now used in a different way, we could say that Atman is the potentiality of light, which is actually darkness, while Buddhi would be the white light. It is the first manifestation of darkness, but not yet differentiated in the colours we see in the world of diversity. Remember, all these examples are relative. Blavatsky explained: 'In using figurative language, as has been done in *The Secret Doctrine*, analogies and comparisons are very frequent. Darkness for instance, as a rule, applies only to the unknown totality, or Absoluteness. Contrasted with eternal darkness, the first Logos is certainly Light; but contrasted with the second or third (the manifested Logos) the first is Darkness, and the others are Light.'[8]

Atman and Buddhi form what is sometimes called 'the dual Monad', which is explained by Blavatsky as follows, 'The [word] Monad is from Greek, 'One' the unit, whatever it is... Atman in reality is not a unit, but the one universal principle, and it is simply a ray. That which uses Buddhi as a vehicle is that ray of that universal principle. Therefore, in reality, it is Buddhi which is the Monad, the one unit.' Atman is the totality beyond any definition, so technically speaking Buddhi is the Monad. However, since Buddhi is the way Atman expresses in the manifested cosmos, we should think of the two principles as one thing - Atma-Buddhi. Suppose you are in one of those dark chambers inside an Egyptian pyramid; to bring the light of the sun into it you must use mirrors. Without the mirrors there is no sunlight in that dark chamber, therefore, from the point of view of those in the chamber, the sunlight and the mirror cannot be separated. Similarly, you can manifest Atman only through Buddhi, and this is why the dual Monad is a single principle.

Blavatsky states, 'Atman and Buddhi cannot be predicated as having anything to do with man, except that man is immersed in them.'[9] She goes on to say, 'So long as he (man) lives, he is overshadowed by these two (Atman and Buddhi); but it is no more the property of that than of anything else.' Sometimes the Monad is described as an individual divine spark giving rise to a human being, but this is not an accurate description for the dual Monad. As Blavatsky says, the Monad 'is not like a seed dropped from a tree, but in its nature is ubiquitous, all-pervading, [and] omnipresent.'[10] The dual Monad is a universal principle, and everything that exists is rooted in it.

What is Buddhi in terms of consciousness? Blavatsky states, 'Buddhi is the consciousness in the universal consciousness, but it is non-consciousness in this world. On this plane of finite consciousness, it is nothing, for it is infinite consciousness.' Since

Atman is described as conscious *non-consciousness*, Buddhi should be regarded as the first principle of sentiency in the cosmos. The possibility of sentient beings exists because of Buddhi. An ant, a plant or even a rock are sentient, in the sense of being able to respond to the environment.

Although Buddhi is infinite consciousness, at this level there is no sense of individuality or agency. As evolution moves through bacteria, plants, and animals, organisms show an increasingly wider ability to respond to the environment and yet, they are not self-conscious. Self-consciousness implies that you are aware of being an individual responding to the environment, but this, as we will see, is a Manasic quality. Beings that are rooted in Atma-Buddhi have a non-self-aware sentiency. They experience the world, but they don't realise they are experiencing it. All of this supports the idea that the dual Monad is a universal (not an individual) principle.

Most of us consider ourselves confined within the body, but we are not our personalities. Ultimately speaking, we are this universal principle - the Monad, which also animates everything around us. This is why there are no boundaries for a mystic. He or she can experience what the stone, the grass, or the bird experience. A conscious experience of our universal nature, however, cannot happen if only Atman and Buddhi are involved - it requires the participation of Manas.

Manas - the Ego

Blavatsky writes in *The Secret Doctrine*, 'Consciousness is ubiquitous and can neither be localized nor centered in any particular subject.' Here, she is talking about the Buddhic root of our consciousness which, as we have seen, is universal. In human beings, however, there is also the principle of Manas to take into account: 'Consciousness per se, as understood and explained by Occult philosophy, is the highest quality of the sentient spiritual principle in us, the Divine Soul (or Buddhi), and our Higher Ego [Manas].'

A special feature of human beings is the presence of an individuality or Ego. The word 'ego' was used by Blavatsky decades before the development of modern psychology with the ideas of Sigmund Freud and others. This word comes

Ego, from the Greek, and it simply means 'I-ness'. Freud used 'ego' to refer to the sense of 'I am this particular person', but besides this personal sense of I-ness, called in Theosophical literature 'lower ego', there are higher expressions of it. Thus, we have terms such as 'Higher Ego' (higher I-ness) and 'Spiritual Ego' (spiritual I-ness). The Higher Ego is a Manasic entity - the human soul that reincarnates in the various bodies.

Walter Gorn Old (20 March 1864 - 29 December 1929), also known as Sepharial, was an astrologer and eminent English Theosophist. He was a member of Blavatsky's Inner Group in London. Talking about the nature of our individuality, Blavatsky asks him, 'Is it your Buddhi, Old, that made you what you are?' Old replies, 'Oh no, it's my Atman;' to which she answers, 'You've got no Atman distinct from any other.' He then goes on to say, 'Well, there is the divine spark in me.' And Blavatsky rebuts, 'No, it is not yours. It is not your divine spark. It is common property. What makes you what you are is your incarnating Ego, that which you were in past lives. That makes you what you are.'

Here, Blavatsky is making an important point. She is telling Walter Gorn Old that he, as the dual Monad (Atma-Buddhi) is the totality, the universal self. When regarding himself as an individuality, he is the reincarnating Ego. In terms of the human principles, Blavatsky states, 'The human Ego is neither Atma nor Buddhi, but the Higher Manas: the intellectual fruition and the efflorescence of the intellectual self-conscious Egotism - in the higher spiritual sense.'[11]

Blavatsky uses the term 'Egotism' here to mean self-awareness, a feeling of I-am-ness. This conscious *sense of being* does not come from Atman or Buddhi but from Manas, which is 'the principle of self-consciousness, the I-am-I.'[12] For Blavatsky, the word 'egotism' is not the same as 'egoism' or selfishness. As she goes on to explain: 'Egoity means 'individuality', never 'personality', and is the opposite of egoism or selfishness.'[13] This is why Blavatsky talks about Higher Manas as being self-consciousness 'in the higher spiritual sense.'

Let us explore this principle of self-consciousness more closely. How do you know that you are here? You know it because there is an awareness of *being present*. This feeling of I-am-ness is a simple knowing that you are, that you exist, without necessarily defining who that 'I' is. Thinking of yourself as being a particular person with a particular history is a limitation imposed on this pure awareness of being, and requires the participation of memory. When we add to the pure sense of being all these concepts about who we are, we have a *sense of identity* - 'I am Mr. Smith'. Now, if you lose your memory, you lose your sense of identity - you don't know who you are. But even if you were not able to remember your name, your appearance, your personal history, etc., you would still know that *you are*. This non-defined awareness of existing is the basis of what Blavatsky calls 'egoity' - the pure sense of being, the simple feeling of I-am-ness. Thus, the Manasic self-awareness (or self-consciousness) has a higher expression in the *impersonal sense of being*, and a lower one in the *personal sense of identity*. Let us now explore the metaphysical foundations for this phenomenon.

The Higher Ego is an entity on the Manasic plane. As such, it is too spiritual to enter into a direct relationship with the physical body, and must do this through what is called 'Lower Manas'. Blavatsky explains it as follows, 'Manas is, as it were, a globe of pure, Divine Light... a unit from a higher sphere, in which is no differentiation. Descending to a plane of differentiation it emanates a Ray which is itself, which it can only manifest through the personality already differentiated. This Ray is the Lower Manas, while the globe of Divine Light, a Kumara on its own plane, is the Higher Ego, or Higher Manas, Manas proper'.[14] According to the Esoteric Philosophy, then, there are two 'egos' in man - on the higher plane, the eternal and impersonal Higher Ego; and on the lower, its Ray, the transient 'personal ego'. The former is the core of our spiritual 'Individuality', and the latter that of the physical 'personality'.

The Ray sent to the personality at the moment of incarnation becomes what we call mind, which is but a shadow of Higher Manas. The latter is omniscient on its own plane, but once it 'has been brought to incarnate on earth, it takes up all the materiality and all the finite attributes, so to say, and the qualities of the personalities it incarnates in'.[15] Thus, although Higher Manas is the source of a pure sense of being, when its ray (Lower Manas) incarnates in the personality, it identifies with the body and develops the personal sense of identity. In practical terms, this means that although we are a spiritual entity, we mistake ourselves with 'this body, emotions and thoughts', and assume that we are this particular person. We thus lock our consciousness within a small fragment of reality and experience ourselves as being separate and limited - an illusion based on an ignorance of who we really are.

The Triple Monad

We can say that, while the dual Monad (Atma-Buddhi) is universal, Higher Manas focuses its light into a single ray, giving rise to an individual centre of consciousness. Thus, the triple Monad (Atma-Buddhi-Manas) is said to be an individuality. This individuality, however, is not separate or essentially different from its universal root.

Imagine a lake that is perfectly still. When circular motion appears and a whirlpool is generated, it is possible to differentiate that local phenomenon from the larger body of water. The whirlpool is not made of anything but the lake's water, and there aren't any molecules of water permanently appropriated by the whirlpool - the water of the lake is constantly moving in and out of it. The only thing that is there, more or less permanently, is a pattern of motion. Thus, the whirlpool can be seen as an 'illusion' produced by the motion of the water and yet, we can talk about the whirlpool as a distinct 'entity' within the lake. In this allegory, Atman is represented by the space the lake occupies, Buddhi is the water, and Manas is the centripetal motion that generates an illusory centre of experience. What we call 'self' is nothing but a whirlpool within universal consciousness. We are the universal consciousness moving through us in a particular pattern (Individuality).

Let us look at this from the point of view of consciousness. As we explained, Atman is beyond the field of consciousness as we know it. It can be said to be conscious non-consciousness. Buddhi is the first manifestation as a universal, non-self-aware consciousness. It is with Manas that we see the rise of conscious self-awareness, by virtue of which this principle becomes a centre of consciousness for the Monad on the lower planes. As Blavatsky says, 'The

[dual] Monad is impersonal and a god per se, albeit unconscious on this plane. For, divorced from its third (often called fifth) principle, Manas, which is the horizontal line of the first manifested triangle or trinity, it can have no consciousness or perception of things on this earthly plane. The highest sees through the eye of the lowest in the manifested world; Purusha (Spirit) remains blind without the help of Prakrit (matter) in the material spheres; and so does Atma-Buddhi without Manas.'[16] Manas brings to the universal Monad the possibility of having a conscious *individual* experience of the cosmos.

Now, Blavatsky asserts that although Atman, Buddhi and Higher Manas are active on the spiritual planes, in most people they do not influence the personal self. The personality, or lower quaternary[17] remains essentially animal in nature, concerning itself with eating, drinking, the search for pleasure, and so on. In other words, although the Monad is our true nature, it will remain 'unmanifested' so long as our self-awareness continues to be stuck on the personal level. For example, Divine Wisdom is a Buddhic state of consciousness where there is direct perception of Truth. We all possess this faculty, but if we cannot be aware at the Buddhic level, we act in ignorance as if there were not Wisdom within ourselves.

Realizing our true universal nature is the goal of human evolution. Blavatsky summarized this journey stating that the Monad 'is universal consciousness, which falling into matter becomes personal consciousness in its last manifestation on earth. And when it gets rid of all the matter that impedes it, when it becomes more and more pure, and it reaches its highest manifestation, or whatever you call it, then it gradually falls into the universal consciousness; it is again reabsorbed into universal consciousness.'

We have explored the gradual 'fall' of Atman into matter manifesting as universal consciousness (Buddhi), then as spiritual self-consciousness (Higher Manas), and finally as personal self-consciousness (Lower Manas). At this point in evolution, Manasic self-consciousness is limited to the lower mind in its association with the physical body and senses. This generates the lower ego, the sense 'I am this body, emotions, and thoughts', which is oblivious of the existence of the Monad. By means of spiritual practice the centre of self-awareness 'turns back', ascending once again through these levels of consciousness from where it came, rising from the lower to Higher Manas, and from there to the Monad.[18] When Manas unites itself with Buddhi, we become aware of a mystic sense of totality - 'I am the whole'. This is a third form of Manasic self-awareness, which Blavatsky called 'Spiritual Ego' or Buddhi-Manas. We are now aware of being the universal Monad even while in the body, which means that the latter is now 'manifested' even on the physical plane.

This is the reason why the human kingdom is so crucial. While the lower kingdoms of nature, being rooted in Atma-Buddhi, experience a unitive state of consciousness, they are not self-aware of it. Only in the human stage, where Manas is awakened, there is the possibility of experiencing consciously the unity of life. We may be able to grasp this better by comparing the experience of a baby and a mystic. Psychology postulates that a baby, before his mind is developed, is unable to appreciate his own separate being, and consequently he feels at one with everything around him. This led some psychologists to maintain that the feeling of unity experienced by mystics constitutes a reversion to a baby-like state. But they are missing a radical difference between a baby and an enlightened being. While the baby is not self-aware in this unitive state, the enlightened being feels *consciously* at one with everything. This illustrates the difference between the dual Monad (Atma-Buddhi) and the fully awakened triple Monad (Atma-Buddhi-Manas).

●

1. Helena Petrovna Blavatsky, *Collected Writings vol XII*, Theosophical Publishing House, 1973.

2. Immanuel Kant (22 April 1724 - 12 February 1804) was an influential Prussian German philosopher in the Age of Enlightenment. In his doctrine of transcendental idealism, he argued that space, time, and causation are mere sensibilities; 'things-in-themselves' exist, but their nature is unknowable. In his view, the mind shapes and structures experience, with all human experience sharing certain structural features. He drew a parallel to the Copernican revolution in his proposition that worldly objects can be intuited a priori ('beforehand'), and that intuition is therefore independent from objective reality.

3. Regarding Blavatsky's use of the word 'man', it is worth noting that 'man' comes from the same root as the Sanskrit 'manu', which means 'the thinker'. From a philosophical point of view, 'man' can be male or female and refers to the entity that has the ability to think. So in Theosophy, the use of the word 'man' is not gendered or sexist.

4. Helena Petrovna Blavatsky, *Collected Writings vol XII*, Theosophical Publishing House, 1973.

5. Helena Petrovna Blavatsky, *The Key to Theosophy*, Theosophical Publishing Company, 1889.

6. Helena Petrovna Blavatsky, *The Secret Doctrine Commentaries*, Theosophical University Press, 1890 and 1891.

7. Ibid.

8. Helena Petrovna Blavatsky, *Collected Writings vol X*, Theosophical Publishing House, 1973.

9. Helena Petrovna Blavatsky, *The Secret Doctrine Commentaries*, Theosophical University Press, 1890 and 1891.

10. Helena Petrovna Blavatsky, *Collected Writings vol V*, Theosophical Publishing House, 1973.

11. Helena Petrovna Blavatsky, *The Secret Doctrine vol II*, Theosophical Publishing Company, London,1888.

12. Helena Petrovna Blavatsky, *Collected Writings vol X*, Theosophical Publishing House, 1973.

13. Helena Petrovna Blavatsky, *The Theosophical Glossary*, The Theosophical Publishing Society, 1892.

14. Helena Petrovna Blavatsky, *Collected Writings vol XII*, Theosophical Publishing House, 1973.

15. Helena Petrovna Blavatsky, *The Secret Doctrine Commentaries*, transactions of the Blavatsky Lodge of the Theosophical Society, Theosophical University Press, 1890 and 1891.

16. Helena Petrovna Blavatsky, *The Secret Doctrine vol II*, Theosophical Publishing Company, London,1888.

17. According to Theosophy, the human being is made up of seven principles. The 'lower quaternary' is a collective term used to describe the four so-called 'lowest' principles. It comprises 'the mental body', 'the astral body', 'the etheric body', and 'the physical body'.

18. Blavatsky recommended practical ways to further this realization, which are beyond the scope of this work. Those interested can learn about this in my book, *Evolution of the Higher Consciousness. An In-depth Study of H. P. Blavatsky's Teachings*. Fohat Productions, 2018.

H. P. Blavatsky

Helena Petrovna Blavatsky was born on 12 August 1831 at Dnepropetrovsk (Ekaterinoslav) in Ukraine. She was the daughter of Colonel Peter Alexeyevich von Hahn and the acclaimed novelist Helena Andreyevna.

Blavatsky was a Russian occultist and author. She founded the Theosophical Society on 17 November 1875 in New York with her co-founders Henry Steel Olcott and William Quan Judge. She described Theosophy as 'the synthesis of science, religion and philosophy'. According to Blavatsky, the Theosophical Society was formed 'to assist in showing to men that such a thing as Theosophy exists, and to help them to ascend towards it by studying and assimilating its eternal verities.'

After publishing her first major work, *Isis Unveiled*, in 1877, she and Henry Steel Olcott moved to India. During their time there, they supported the struggle to re-establish Indian philosophical and religious ideas. Blavatsky also began publishing and editing a magazine called *The Theosophist*. She and Olcott set up the international headquarters of the Theosophical Society in Adyar, Chennai, India. In 1885, Blavatsky left India for Europe, where she continued her work developing the Theosophical Society. She settled in London, England in 1887, establishing Blavatsky Lodge and launching a new magazine called *Lucifer* (the light-bringer).

Her second major work, *The Secret Doctrine*, was published in 1888. In the same year, with the help of William Quan Judge, she established the Esoteric Section of The Theosophical Society. In 1889, she published two further works, *The Key to Theosophy* and *The Voice of the Silence*. The following year, she inaugurated the new European headquarters of the Theosophical Society in London. After a long period of ill health, Helena Blavatsky died of influenza in London on 8 May 1891. The date has been commemorated by Theosophists ever since as White Lotus Day.

Kosmic Mind
by H. P. Blavatsky (1890)

Whatsoever quits the Laya (homogeneous) state, becomes active conscious life. Individual consciousness emanates from, and returns into Absolute consciousness, which is eternal MOTION.

THE SECRET DOCTRINE VOL I

Whatever that be which thinks, which understands, which wills, which acts, it is something celestial and divine, and upon that account must necessarily be eternal.

MARCUS TULLIUS CICERO

Edison's conception of matter was quoted in our March editorial article. The great American electrician is reported by Mr. G. Parsons Lathrop in *Harper's Magazine* as giving out his personal belief about the atoms being 'possessed by a certain amount of intelligence,' and shown indulging in other reveries of this kind. For this flight of fancy the February *Review of Reviews* takes the inventor of the phonograph to task and critically remarks that 'Edison is much given to dreaming,' his 'scientific imagination' being constantly at work.

Would to goodness the men of science exercised their 'scientific imagination' a little more and their dogmatic and cold negations a little less. Dreams differ. In that strange state of being which, as Byron has it, puts us in a position 'with seal'd eyes to see,' one often perceives more real facts than when awake. Imagination is, again, one of the strongest elements in human nature, or in the words of Dugald Stewart[1] it 'is the great spring of human activity, and the principal source of human improvement... Destroy the faculty, and the condition of men will become as stationary as that of the brutes'. It is the best guide of our blind senses, without which the latter could never lead us beyond matter and its illusions. The greatest discoveries of modern science are due to the imaginative faculty of the discoverers. But when has anything new been postulated, when a theory clashing with and contradicting a comfortably settled predecessor put forth, without orthodox science first sitting on it, and trying to crush it out of existence? Harvey[2] was also regarded at first as a 'dreamer and a madman to boot'. Finally, the whole of modern science is formed of 'working hypotheses', the fruits of 'scientific imagination' as Mr. Tyndall[3] felicitously called it.

Is it then, because consciousness in every universal atom and the possibility of a complete control over the cells and atoms of his body by man, have not been honored so far with the imprimatur of the Popes of exact science, that the idea is to be dismissed as a dream? Occultism gives the same teaching. Occultism tells us that every atom, like the monad of Leibnitz,[4] is a little universe in itself; and that every organ and cell in the human body is endowed with a brain of its own, with memory, therefore, experience and discriminative powers.

The idea of Universal Life composed of individual atomic lives is one of the oldest teachings of esoteric philosophy, and the very modern hypothesis of modern science, that of crystalline life, is the first ray from the ancient luminary of knowledge that has reached our scholars. If plants can be shown to have nerves and sensations and instinct (but another word for consciousness), why not allow the same in the cells of the human body? Science divides matter into organic and inorganic bodies, only because it rejects the idea of absolute life and a life-principle as an entity: otherwise it would be the first to see that absolute life cannot produce even a geometrical point, or an atom inorganic in its essence. But Occultism, you see, 'teaches mysteries' they say; and mystery is the negation of common sense, just as again metaphysics is but a kind of poetry, according to Mr. Tyndall. There is no such thing for science as mystery; and therefore, as a Life Principle is, and must remain for the intellects of our civilized races for ever a mystery on physical lines - they who deal in this question have to be of necessity either fools or knaves. *Dixit*. Nevertheless, we may repeat with a French preacher:[5] 'mystery is the fatality of science'. Official science is surrounded on every side and hedged in by unapproachable, for ever impenetrable mysteries. And why? Simply because physical science is self-doomed to a squirrel-like progress around a wheel of matter limited by our five senses. And though it is as confessedly ignorant of the formation of matter, as of the generation of a simple cell; though it is as powerless to explain what is this, that, or the other, it will yet dogmatize and insist on what life, matter and the rest are not. It comes to this: the words of Father Felix addressed fifty years ago to the French academicians have nearly become immortal as a truism. 'Gentlemen,' he said, 'you throw into our teeth the reproach that we teach mysteries. But imagine whatever science you will; follow the magnificent sweep of its deductions... and when you arrive at its parent source you come face to face with the unknown!'

Now to lay at rest once for all in the minds of Theosophists this vexed question, we intend to prove that modern science, owing to physiology, is itself on the eve of discovering that consciousness is universal - thus justifying Edison's 'dreams.' But before we do this, we mean also to show that though many a man of science is soaked through and through with such belief, very few are brave enough to openly admit it, as the late Dr. Pirogov[6] of St. Petersburg has done in his posthumous Memoirs. Indeed that great surgeon and pathologist raised by their publication quite a howl of indignation among his colleagues. How then? the public asked: He, Dr. Pirogov, whom we regarded as almost the embodiment of European learning, believing in the superstitions of crazy alchemists? He, who in the words of a contemporary, 'was the very incarnation of exact science and methods of thought; who had dissected hundreds and thousands of human organs, making himself thus acquainted with all the mysteries of surgery and anatomy as we are with our familiar furniture; the savant for whom physiology had no secrets and who, above all men, was one to whom Voltaire might have ironically asked whether he had not found the immortal soul between the bladder and the blind gut, - that same Pirogov is found after his death devoting whole chapters in his literary Will to the scientific demonstration...[7] Of what? Why, of the existence in every organism of a distinct 'VITAL FORCE' independent of any physical or chemical process. Like Liebig[8] he accepted the derided and tabooed homogeneity of nature - a Life Principle - that persecuted and hapless teleology, or the science of the final causes of things, which is as philosophical as it is unscientific, if we have to believe imperial and royal academies. His unpardonable sin in the eyes of dogmatic modern science, however, was this: the great anatomist and surgeon had the 'hardihood' to declare in his Memoirs, that 'we have no cause to reject the possibility of the existence of organisms endowed with such properties that would impart to them - the direct embodiment of the universal mind - a perfection inaccessible to our own (human) mind... Because, we have no right to maintain that man is the last expression of the divine creative thought'.

Such are the chief features of the heresy of one, who ranked high among the men of exact science of his age. His Memoirs show plainly that not only he believed in Universal Deity, divine Ideation, or the Hermetic 'Thought divine,' as a Vital Principle, but taught all this, and tried to demonstrate it scientifically. Thus he argues that

Universal Mind needs no physico-chemical, or mechanical brain as an organ of transmission. He even goes so far as to admit it in these suggestive words: 'Our reason must accept in all necessity an infinite and eternal Mind which rules and governs the ocean of life... Thought and creative ideation, in full agreement with the laws of unity and causation, manifest themselves plainly enough in universal life without the participation of brain-slush... Directing the forces and elements toward the formation of organisms, this organizing life-principle becomes self-sentient, self-conscious, racial or individual. Substance, ruled and directed by the life-principle, is organised according to a general defined plan into certain types...'

He explains this belief by confessing that never, during his long life so full of study, observation, and experiments, could he 'acquire the conviction, that our brain could be the only organ of thought in the whole universe, that everything in this world, save that organ, should be unconditioned and senseless, and that human thought alone should impart to the universe a meaning and a reasonable harmony in its integrity'.

And he adds à propos of Moleschott's[9] materialism: 'Howsoever much fish and peas I may eat, never shall I consent to give away my Ego into durance vile of a product casually extracted by modern alchemy from the urine.[10] If, in our conceptions of the Universe it be our fate to fall into illusions, then my 'illusion' has, at least, the advantage of being very consoling. For it shows to me an intelligent Universe and the activity of Forces working in it harmoniously and intelligently; and that my 'I' is not the product of chemical and histological elements but an embodiment of a common universal Mind. The latter, I sense and represent to myself as acting in free will and consciousness in accordance with the same laws which are traced for the guidance of my own mind, but only exempt from that restraint which trammels our human conscious individuality.'

For, as remarks elsewhere this great and philosophic man of Science: 'The limitless and the eternal, is not only a postulate of our mind and reason, but also a gigantic fact, in itself. What would become of our ethical or moral principle were not the everlasting and integral truth to serve it as a foundation!' The above selections translated verbatim from the confessions of one who was during his long life a star of the first magnitude in the fields of pathology and surgery, show him imbued and soaked through with the philosophy of a reasoned and scientific mysticism. In reading the Memoirs of that man of scientific fame, we feel proud of finding him accepting, almost wholesale, the fundamental doctrines and beliefs of Theosophy. With such an exceptionally scientific mind in the ranks of mystics, the idiotic grins, the cheap satires and flings at our great Philosophy by some European and American 'Freethinkers' become almost a compliment. More than ever do they appear to us like the frightened discordant cry of the night- owl hurrying to hide in its dark ruins before the light of the morning Sun.

The progress of physiology itself, as we have just said, is a sure warrant that the dawn of that day when a full recognition of a universally diffused mind will be an accomplished fact, is not far off. It is only a question of time.

For, notwithstanding the boast of physiology, that the aim of its researches is only the summing up of every vital function in order to bring them into a definite order by showing their mutual relations to, and connection with, the laws of physics and chemistry, hence, in their final form with mechanical laws - we fear there is a good deal of contradiction between the confessed object and the speculations of some of the best of our modern physiologists. While few of them would dare to return as openly as did Dr. Pirogov to the 'exploded superstition' of vitalism and the severely exiled life principle, the principium vitæ of Paracelsus[11] - yet physiology stands sorely perplexed in the face of its ablest representatives before certain facts. Unfortunately for us, this age of ours is not conducive to the development of moral courage. The time for most to act on the noble idea of 'principia non homines',[12] has not yet come. And yet there are exceptions to the general rule, and physiology - whose destiny it is to become the hand-maiden of Occult truths - has not let the latter remain without their witnesses. There are those who are already stoutly protesting against certain hitherto favorite propositions. For instance, some physiologists are already denying that it is the forces and substances of so-called 'inanimate' nature, which are acting exclusively in living beings. For, as they well argue: 'The fact that we reject the interference of other forces in living things, depends entirely on the limitations of our senses. We use, indeed, the same organs for our observations of both animate and inanimate nature; and these organs can receive manifestations of only a limited realm of motion. Vibrations passed along the fibres of our optic nerves to the brain reach our perceptions through our consciousness as sensations of light and color; vibrations affecting our consciousness through our auditory organs strike us as sounds; all our feelings, through whichever of our senses, are due to nothing but motions.'

Such are the teachings of physical Science, and such were in their roughest outlines those of Occultism, æons and millenniums back. The difference, however, and most vital distinction between the two teachings, is this: official science sees in motion simply a blind, unreasoning force or law; Occultism, tracing motion to its origin, identifies it with the Universal Deity, and calls this eternal ceaseless motion - the 'Great Breath'.[13]

Nevertheless, however limited the conception of modern science about the said Force, still it is suggestive enough to have forced the following remark from a great scientist, the present professor of physiology at the University of Basle,[14] who speaks like an occultist: 'It would be folly in us to expect to be ever able to discover, with the assistance only of our external senses, in animate nature that something which we are unable to find in the inanimate.'

And forthwith the lecturer adds that man being endowed 'in addition to his physical senses with an inner sense', a perception which gives him the possibility of observing the states and phenomena of his own consciousness, 'he has to use that in dealing with animate nature' - a profession of faith verging suspiciously on the borders of Occultism. He denies, moreover, the assumption, that the states and phenomena of consciousness represent in substance the same manifestations of motion as in the external world, and bases his denial by the reminder that not all of such states and manifestations have necessarily a spatial extension. According to him that only is connected with our conception of space which has reached our consciousness through sight, touch, and the muscular sense, while all the other senses, all the effects, tendencies, as all the interminable series of representations, have no extension in space, but only in time.

Thus he asks: 'Where then is there room in this for a mechanical theory? Objectors might argue that this is so only in appearance, while in reality all these have a spatial extension. But such an argument would be entirely erroneous. Our sole reason for believing that objects perceived by the senses have such extension in the external world, rests on the idea that they seem to do so, as far as they can be watched and observed through the senses of sight and touch. With regard, however, to the realm of our inner senses even that supposed foundation loses its force and there is no ground for admitting it.'

The winding up argument of the lecturer is most interesting to Theosophists. Says this physiologist of the modern school of Materialism: 'Thus, a deeper and more direct acquaintance with our inner nature unveils to us a world entirely unlike the world represented to us by our external senses, and reveals the most heterogeneous faculties, shows objects having nought to do with spatial extension, and phenomena absolutely disconnected with those that fall under mechanical laws.'

Hitherto, the opponents of vitalism and 'life-principle', as well as the followers of the mechanical theory of life, based their views on the supposed fact, that, as physiology was progressing forward, its students succeeded more and more in connecting its functions with the laws of blind matter. All those manifestations that used to be attributed to a 'mystical life-force', they said, may be brought now under physical and chemical laws. And they were, and still are loudly clamoring for the recognition of the fact that it is only a question of time when it will be triumphantly demonstrated that the whole vital process, in its grand totality, represents nothing more mysterious than a very complicated phenomenon of motion, exclusively governed by the forces of inanimate nature.

But here we have a professor of physiology who asserts that the history of physiology proves, unfortunately for them, quite the contrary; and he pronounces these ominous words: 'I maintain that the more our experiments and observations are exact and many-sided, the deeper we penetrate into facts, the more we try to fathom and speculate on the phenomena of life, the more we acquire the conviction that even those phenomena that we had hoped to be already able to explain by physical and chemical laws, are in reality unfathomable. They are vastly more complicated, in fact; and as we stand at present, they will not yield to any mechanical explanation.'

This is a terrible blow at the puffed-up bladder known as Materialism, which is as empty as it is dilated. A Judas in the camp of the apostles of negation - the 'animalists'! But the Basle professor is no solitary exception, as we have just shown; and there are several physiologists who are of his way of thinking; indeed some of them going so far as to almost accept free-will and consciousness, in the simplest monadic protoplasms!

One discovery after the other tends in this direction. The works of some German physiologists are especially interesting with regard to cases of consciousness and positive discrimination - one is almost inclined to say thought - in the Amœbae. Now the Amœbae or animalculae are, as all know, microscopical protoplasms - as the *Vampyrello Spirogyra* for instance, a most simple elementary cell, a protoplasmic drop, formless and almost structureless. And yet it shows in its behavior something for which zoologists, if they do not call it mind and power of reasoning, will have to find some other qualification, and coin a new term. For see what Cienkowsky[15] says of it. Speaking of this microscopical, bare, reddish cell he describes the way in which it hunts for and finds among a number of other aquatic plants one called *Spirogyra*, rejecting every other food. Examining its peregrinations under a powerful microscope, he found it when moved by hunger, first projecting its *pseudopodiæ* (false feet) by the help of which it crawls. Then it commences moving about until among a great variety of plants it comes across a *Spirogyra*, after which it proceeds toward the cellulated portion of one of the cells of the latter, and placing itself on it, it bursts the tissue, sucks the contents of one cell and then passes on to another, repeating the same process. This naturalist never saw it take any other food, and it never touched any of the numerous plants placed by Cienkowsky in its way. Mentioning another Amoeba - the *Colpadella Pugnax* - he says that he found it showing the same predilection for the *Chlamydomonas* on which it feeds exclusively; 'having made a puncture in the body of the Chlamydomonas it sucks its chlorophyll and then goes away', he writes, adding these significant words: 'The way of acting of these monads during their search for and reception of food, is so amazing that one is almost inclined to see in them consciously acting beings!'

Not less suggestive are the observations of Th. W. Engelmann[16] (Beiträge zur Physiologie des Protoplasm), on the *Arcella*, another unicellular organism only a trifle more complex than the *Vampyrella*. He shows them in a drop of water under a microscope on a piece of glass, lying so to speak, on their backs, i.e., on their convex side, so that the *pseudopodiæ*, projected from the edge of the shell, find no hold in space and leave the Amoeba helpless. Under these circumstances the following curious fact is observed. Under the very edge of one of the sides of the protoplasm gas-bubbles begin immediately to form, which, making that side lighter, allow it to be raised, bringing at the same time the opposite side of the creature into contact with the glass, thus furnishing its *pseudo* or false feet means to get hold of the surface and thereby turning over its body to raise itself on all its *pseudopodiæ*. After this, the Amoeba proceeds to suck back into itself the gas-bubbles and begins to move. If a like drop of water is placed on the lower extremity of the glass, then following the law of gravity the Amoeba will find themselves at first at the lower end of the drop of water. Failing to find there a point of support, they proceed to generate large bubbles of gas, when, becoming lighter than the water, they are raised up to the surface of the drop.

In the words of Engelmann: 'If having reached the surface of the glass they find no more support for their feet than before, forthwith one sees the gas-globules diminishing on one side and increasing in size and number on the other, or both, until the creatures touch with the edge of their shell the surface of the glass, and are enabled to turn over. No sooner is this done than the gas-globules disappear and the *Arcellae* begin crawling. Detach them carefully by means of a fine needle from the surface of the glass and thus bring them down once more to the lower surface of the drop of water; and forthwith they will repeat the same process, varying its details according to necessity and devising new means to reach their desired aim. Try as much as you will to place them in uncomfortable positions, and they find means to extricate themselves from them, each time, by one device or the other; and no sooner have they succeeded than the gas-bubbles disappear! It is impossible not to admit that such facts as these point to the presence of some PSYCHIC process in the protoplasm.'[17]

Among hundreds of accusations against Asiatic nations of degrading superstitions, based on 'crass ignorance', there exists no more serious denunciation than that which accuses and convicts them of personifying and even deifying the chief organs of, and in, the human body. Indeed, do not we hear these 'benighted fools' of Hindus speaking of the small-pox as a goddess - thus personifying the microbes of the variolic virus? Do we not read about *Tantrikas*, a sect of mystics, giving proper names to nerves, cells and arteries, connecting and identifying various parts of the body with deities, endowing functions and physiological processes with intelligence, and what not? The vertebrae, fibres, ganglia, the cord, etc., of the spinal column; the heart, its four chambers, auricle and ventricle, valves and the rest; stomach, liver, lungs and spleen, everything has its special deific name, is believed to act consciously and to act under the potent will of the Yogi, whose head and heart are the seats of Brahmâ and the various parts of whose body are all the pleasure grounds of this or another deity!

This is indeed ignorance. Especially when we think that the said organs, and the whole body of man are composed of cells, and these cells are now being recognized as individual organisms and - *quien sabe*[18] - will come perhaps to be recognized some day as an independent race of thinkers inhabiting the globe, called man! It really looks like it. For was it not hitherto believed that all the phenomena of assimilation and sucking in of food by the intestinal canal, could be explained by the laws of diffusion and endosmosis? And now, alas, physiologists have come to learn that the action of the intestinal canal during the act of absorbing, is not identical with the action of the non-living membrane in the dialyser. It is now well demonstrated that: 'This wall is covered with epithelium cells, each of which is an organism *per se*, a living being, and with very complex functions. We know further, that such a cell assimilates food - by means of active contractions of its protoplasmic body - in a manner as mysterious as that which we notice in the independent Amoebae and animalculae. We can observe on the intestinal epithelium of the cold-blooded animals how these cells project shoots - *pseudopodiae* - out of their contractive, bare, protoplasmic bodies - which *pseudopodiæ*, or false feet, fish out of the food drops of fat, suck them into their protoplasm and send it further, toward the lymph-duct... The lymphatic cells issuing from the nests of the adipose tissue, and squeezing themselves through the epithelium cells up to the surface of the intestines, absorb therein the drops of fat and loaded with their prey, travel homeward to the lymphatic canals. So long as this active work of the cells remained unknown to us, the fact that while the globules of fat penetrated through the walls of the intestines into lymphatic channels, the smallest of pigmental grains introduced into the intestines did not do so, - remained unexplained. But today we know, that this faculty of selecting their special food - of assimilating the useful and rejecting the useless and the harmful - is common to all the unicellular organisms.'[19]

And the lecturer queries, why, if this discrimination in the selection of food exists in the simplest and most elementary of the cells, in the formless and structureless protoplasmic drops - why it should not exist also in the epithelium cells of our intestinal canal. Indeed, if the *Vampyrella* recognizes its much beloved *Spirogyra,* among hundreds of other plants as shown above, why should not the epithelian cell, sense, choose and select its favorite drop of fat from a pigmental grain? But we will be told that 'sensing, choosing and selecting' pertain only to reasoning beings, at least to the instinct of more structural animals than is the protoplasmic cell outside or inside man. Agreed; but as we translate from the lecture of a learned physiologist and the works of other learned naturalists, we can only say, that these learned gentlemen must know what they are talking about; though they are probably ignorant of the fact that their scientific prose is but one degree removed from the ignorant, superstitious, but rather poetical 'twaddle' of the Hindu Yogis and Tantrikas.

Anyhow, our professor of physiology falls foul of the materialistic theories of diffusion and endosmosis. Armed with the facts of the evident discrimination and a mind in the cells, he demonstrates by numerous instances the fallacy of trying to explain certain physiological processes by mechanical theories; such for instance as the passing of sugar from the liver (where it is transformed into glucose) into the blood. Physiologists find great difficulty in explaining this process, and regard it as an impossibility to bring it under the endosmosic laws. In all probability the lymphatic cells play just as active a part during the absorption of alimentary substances dissolved in water, as the peptics do, a process well demonstrated by F. Hofmeister.[20] Generally speaking, poor convenient endosmose is dethroned and exiled from among the active functionaries of the human body as a useless sinecurist. It has lost its voice in the matter of glands and other agents of secretion, in the action of which the same epithelium cells have replaced it. The mysterious faculties of selection, of extracting from the blood one kind of substance and rejecting another, of transforming the former by means of decomposition and synthesis, of directing some of the products into passages which will throw them out of the body and redirecting others into lymphatic and blood vessels - such is the work of the cells. 'It is evident that in all this there is not the slightest hint at diffusion or endosmose,' says the Basle physiologist. 'It becomes entirely useless to try and explain these phenomena by chemical laws.'

But perhaps physiology is luckier in some other department? Failing in the laws of alimentation it may have found some consolation for its mechanical theories in the question of the activity of muscles and nerves, which it sought to explain by electric laws? Alas, save in a few fishes - in no other living organisms, least of all in the human body, could it find any possibility of pointing out electric currents as the chief ruling agency. Electro-biology on the lines of pure dynamic electricity has egregiously failed. Ignorant of 'Fohat' no electrical currents suffice to explain to it either muscular or nervous activity!

But there is such a thing as the physiology of external sensations. Here we are no longer on *terra incognita*, and all such phenomena have already found purely physical explanations. No doubt there is the phenomenon of sight, the eye with its optical apparatus, its camera obscura. But the fact of the sameness of the reproduction of things in the eye, according to the same laws of refraction as on the plate of a photographic machine, is no vital phenomenon. The same may be reproduced on a dead eye. The phenomenon of life consists in the evolution and development of the eye itself. How is this marvellous and complicated work produced? To this Physiology replies, 'We do not know'; for, toward the solution of this great problem: 'Physiology has not yet made one single step. True, we can follow the sequence of the stages of the development and formation of the eye, but why it is so and what is the causal connection, we have absolutely no idea. The second vital phenomenon of the eye is its accommodating activity. And here we are again face to face with the functions of nerves and muscles - our old insoluble riddles. The same may be said of all the organs of sense. The same also relates to other departments of physiology. We had hoped to explain the phenomena of the circulation of the blood by the laws of hydrostatics or hydrodynamics. Of course the blood moves in accordance with the hydrodynamical laws; but its relation to them remains utterly passive. As to the active functions of the heart and the muscles of its vessels, no one, so far, has ever been able to explain them by physical laws.'

The underlined words in the concluding portion of the able Professor's lecture are worthy of an Occultist. Indeed, he seems to be repeating an aphorism from the 'Elementary Instructions' of the esoteric physiology of practical Occultism: 'The riddle of life is found in the active functions of a living organism,[21] the real perception of which activity we can get only through self-observation, and not owing to our external senses; by observations on our will, so far as it penetrates our consciousness, thus revealing itself to our inner sense. Therefore, when the same phenomenon acts only on our external senses, we recognize it no longer. We see everything that takes place around and near the phenomenon of motion, but the essence of that phenomenon we do not see at all, because we lack for it a special organ of receptivity. We can accept that *esse*[22] in a mere hypothetical way, and do so, in fact, when we speak of 'active functions'. Thus does every physiologist, for he cannot go on without such hypothesis; and this is a first experiment of a psychological explanation of all vital phenomena... And if it is demonstrated to us that we are unable with the help only of physics and chemistry to explain the phenomena of life, what may we expect from other adjuncts of physiology, from the sciences of morphology, anatomy, and histology? I maintain that these can never help us to unriddle the problem of any of the mysterious phenomena of life. For after we have succeeded with the help of scalpel and microscope in dividing the organisms into their most elementary compounds, and reached the simplest of cells, it is just here that we find ourselves face to face with the greatest problem of all. The simplest monad, a microscopical point of protoplasm, formless and

Proto Plasma

structureless, exhibits yet all the essential vital functions, alimentation, growth, breeding, motion, feeling and sensuous perception, and even such functions which replace 'consciousness' - the soul of the higher animals!'

The problem - for Materialism - is a terrible one, indeed! Shall our cells, and infinitesimal monads in nature, do for us that which the arguments of the greatest Pantheistic philosophers have hitherto failed to do? Let us hope so. And if they do, then the 'superstitious and ignorant' Eastern Yogis, and even their exoteric followers, will find themselves vindicated. For we hear from the same physiologist that: 'A large number of poisons are prevented by the epithelium cells from penetrating into lymphatic spaces, though we know that they are easily decomposed in the abdominal and intestinal juices. More than this. Physiology is aware that by injecting these poisons directly into the blood, they will separate from, and reappear through the intestinal walls, and that in this process the lymphatic cells take a most active part.'

If the reader turns to *Webster's Dictionary* he will find therein a curious explanation at the words 'lymphatic' and 'lymph'. Etymologists think that the Latin word *lympha* is derived from the Greek *nymphe*, 'a nymph or inferior Goddess', they say. 'The Muses were sometimes called nymphs by the poets. Hence (according to Webster) all persons in a state of rapture, as seers, poets, madmen, etc., were said to be caught by the nymphs.'

The Goddess of Moisture (the Greek and Latin *nymph* or *lymph*, then) is fabled in India as being born from the pores of one of the Gods, whether the Ocean God, Varuna, or a minor 'River God' is left to the particular sect and fancy of the believers. But the main question is, that the ancient Greeks and Latins are thus admittedly known to have shared in the same 'superstitions' as the Hindus. This superstition is shown in their maintaining to this day that every atom of matter in the four (or five) Elements is an emanation from an inferior God or Goddess, himself or herself an earlier emanation from a superior deity; and, moreover, that each of these atoms - being Brahmâ, one of whose names is *Anu*, or atom - no sooner is it emanated than it becomes endowed with consciousness, each of its kind, and free-will, acting

Atma ?

within the limits of law. Now, he who knows that the *kosmic trimurti* (trinity) composed of Brahmâ, the Creator; Vishnu, the Preserver; and Siva, the Destroyer, is a most magnificent and scientific symbol of the material Universe and its gradual evolution; and who finds a proof of this, in the etymology of the names of these deities,[23] plus the doctrines of *Gupta Vidya,* or esoteric knowledge - knows also how to correctly understand this 'superstition'. The five fundamental titles of Vishnu - added to that of *Anu* (atom), common to all the trimurtic personages - which are, *Bhutâtman,* one with the created or emanated materials of the world; *Pradhanâtman,* 'one with the senses'; *Paramâtman,* 'Supreme Soul'; and Atman, Kosmic Soul, or the Universal Mind - show sufficiently what the ancient Hindus meant by endowing with mind and consciousness every atom and giving it a distinct name of a God or a Goddess. Place their Pantheon, composed of 30 crores (or 300 millions) of deities within the macrocosm (the Universe), or inside the microcosm (man), and the number will not be found overrated, since they relate to the atoms, cells, and molecules of everything that is.

This, no doubt, is too poetical and abstruse for our generation, but it seems decidedly as scientific, if not more so, than the teachings derived from the latest discoveries of Physiology and Natural History.

1. Dugald Stewart FRSE FRS (22 November 1753 - 11 June 1828) was a Scottish philosopher and mathematician. He was a major exponent of the Scottish 'common sense' school of philosophy. His major work is *Elements of the Philosophy of the Human Mind*, 3 vol (1792, 1814, and 1827). In 1783 he was a joint founder of the Royal Society of Edinburgh.

2. William Harvey (1 April 1578 - 3 June 1657) was an English physician and the first to describe the circulatory system in detail. His theory was at odds with the accepted beliefs of the time and caused controversy.

3. John Tyndall (2 August 1820 - 4 December 1893) was a prominent 19th-century Irish physicist. He came to fame in the 1850s with his study of diamagnetism. Later he made discoveries relating to infrared radiation and the physical properties of air. From 1853 to 1887 he was professor of physics at the Royal Institution of Great Britain in London.

4. Gottfried Wilhelm (von) Leibniz, sometimes spelled Leibnitz, (1 July 1646 - 14 November 1716) was a prominent German polymath and one of the most important logicians, mathematicians and natural philosophers of the Enlightenment. His best known contribution to metaphysics is his theory of monads. He proposes that the universe is made of an infinite number of simple substances known as monads, which are the 'ultimate units of existence in nature'.

5. Célestin Joseph Félix (28 June 1810 - 7 July 1891), French Jesuit.

6. Nikolay Ivanovich Pirogov (25 November 1810 - 5 December 1881) was a prominent Russian scientist, medical doctor, pedagogue, public figure, and corresponding member of the Russian Academy of Sciences (1847). He is considered to be the founder of field surgery, and was one of the first surgeons in Europe to use ether as an anaesthetic.

7. Novoye Vremya was a Russian newspaper published in St. Petersburg from 1868 to 1917.

8. Justus Freiherr von Liebig (12 May 1803 - 18 April 1873) was a German scientist who made major contributions to agricultural and biological chemistry.

9. Jacob Moleschott (9 August 1822 - 20 May 1893) was a Dutch physiologist and writer on dietetics. He was a member of the German Academy of Sciences.

10. Just as kidneys produce urine, the brain produces mind, as Jacob Moleschott so inimitably put it.

11. Paracelsus (1493/4 - 24 September 1541), born Theophrastus von Hohenheim (full name Philippus Aureolus Theophrastus Bombastus von Hohenheim), was a Swiss physician, alchemist and astrologer of the German Renaissance. He was a pioneer in several aspects of the 'medical revolution' of the Renaissance, emphasising the value of observation. He is credited as the 'father of toxicology'.

12. Principles, not men.

13. See *The Secret Doctrine vol I.*

14. Johann Friedrich Miescher (1844 - 1895) was a Swiss chemist
and physiologist and Professor of Physiology at Basel
University from 1871-1895. According to Blavatsky, she is
quoting 'from a paper read by him some time ago at a
public lecture'.

15. Leon Cienkowski aka Lev Semyonovich Tsenkovsky (1 October
1822 - 25 September 1887) was a Polish-Ukrainian botanist,
protozoologist, bacteriologist, and a corresponding member of
the Saint Petersburg Academy of Sciences. See his work *Beiträge
zur Kentniss der Monaden* (Archiv für Anatomie und Physiologie).

16. Theodor Wilhelm Engelmann (14 November 1843 - 20 May
1909) was a German botanist, physiologist, microbiologist and
Professor of Physiology. In 1881, he observed the movement of
bacteria towards the chloroplasts in a strand of *Spirogyra* algae.
He hypothesized that the bacteria were moving in response to
oxygen generated by the photosynthetically active chloroplasts
in the algae.

17. See Pflüger's Archiv (*European Journal of Physiology*) Bd. II,
S. 387.

18. Who Knows.

19. From the paper read by Johann Miescher, Professor of
Physiology, University of Basle, previously quoted.

20. Franz Hofmeister (30 August 1850 - 26 July 1922) was an early
protein scientist, known for his studies of salts that influence the
solubility and conformational stability of proteins. See his work
*Untersuchungen über Resorption und Assimilation der Nährstoffe /
Studies on absorption and the Assimilation of nutrients* (Archiv für
Experimentale Pathologie, Bk. XIX, 1885.)

21. Life and activity are but two different names for the same idea, or, what is still more correct, they are two words with which the men of science connect no definite idea whatever. Nevertheless, and perhaps just for that, they are obliged to use them, for they contain the point of contact between the most difficult problems over which, in fact, the greatest thinkers of the materialistic school have ever tripped. (H.P. Blavatsky footnote.)

22. Essential nature.

23. Brahma comes from the root brih, to 'expand', to 'scatter', Vishnu, from the root vis or vish (phonetically) 'to enter into', 'to pervade' - the Universe of matter. As to Siva - the patron of the yogis - the etymology of his name would remain incomprehensible to the casual reader. (H.P. Blavatsky footnote.)